ANTHRAX

SAFE WORKING AND THE PREVENTION OF INFECTION

HSE BOOKS

This guidance is issued by the Health and Safety Executive. Following the guidance is not compulsory and you are free to take other action. But if you do follow the guidance you will normally be doing enough to comply with the law. Health and safety inspectors seek to secure compliance with the law and may refer to this guidance as illustrating good practice.

Further information about this guidance may be obtained from:

Directorate of Science and Technology E6

Magdalen House

Stanley Precinct

Bootle

Merseyside L20 3QZ

CONTENTS

PREFACE

HSE has previously published guidance on anthrax in 1979 and this publication supersedes that document Guidance Note EH23 *Anthrax: health hazards.*

This booklet provides information on anthrax and where it may present a risk to workers. It also gives advice on how risks of exposure to anthrax may be prevented or minimised, and practical measures to achieve adequate control in the workplace.

BACKGROUND INFORMATION

What is anthrax?

1   Anthrax is a potentially fatal infection caused by the bacterium *Bacillus anthracis*. It is a zoonosis, a disease that is transmitted from animals to humans, and primarily affects herbivorous animals, although all other mammals may be susceptible. The main reservoirs of the disease are cattle, horses, goats, sheep and pigs. Animals become infected by the consumption of contaminated water, hay or by grazing on contaminated land, and through contaminated feedstuffs, eg bonemeal. Direct transmission between living animals is not thought to occur. Humans become at risk of incidental infection through contact with diseased animals, their secretions, hides, hair or other products.

2   Anthrax can occur in humans in a number of forms, although it is rare in the UK. The most common type affects the skin and accounts for more than 95% of all cases. Other types are inhalation or pulmonary anthrax, and ingestion or intestinal anthrax.

How anthrax infection is spread to humans

3   The routes of transmission of anthrax may be through:

▼   skin lesions (cuts and abrasions) or puncture;
▼   inhalation;
▼   ingestion.

If an animal dies of anthrax and is buried immediately, without opening the carcass or skinning, then the bacteria, retained within the animal's blood, will also die. However, a diseased animal will often bleed through its openings before dying, liberating large numbers of anthrax organisms. When the infected blood comes into contact with air, the bacteria form spores which may persist in the environment for many years. For humans to contract anthrax, exposure to large numbers of the organism is thought to be essential.

4 Skin contact may result in cutaneous anthrax. This is contracted by handling material containing spores from infected animals, the products of these animals, or from the contaminated environment. Similarly, inhalation anthrax can develop from breathing in spore-laden material. Biting flies can carry the anthrax organism. The disease has also been transmitted indirectly through poor hygiene in working practices, during post-mortem procedures and washing contaminated clothing. Ingestion anthrax occurs through eating meat from infected animals.

Prevalence of anthrax

UK

5 Human cases of anthrax are now exceedingly rare in the UK. Since 1981 there have been 17 human cases notified and no fatalities. In August 1995 one case of cutaneous anthrax was diagnosed in someone in London who had worked in the leather industry, although the occupational link was not proven. The last confirmed case before this was in 1991 in a woollen industry worker in Scotland. This contrasts with figures for the beginning of the century when in the period between 1899 and 1912 there were 354 cases of anthrax. Figure 1 illustrates the declining incidence of the disease throughout this century. Small outbreaks continue to occur annually in livestock (see Table 1).

World

6 Data on the worldwide occurrence of human anthrax are limited but most reported cases occur in Africa, the Middle East and southern Asia. The disease is known to be a major cause of livestock mortality in certain countries where anthrax is endemic. However, this information may also be restricted as most of the world takes little account of anthrax in sheep and goats, attention being centred more on cattle. Consequently, statements about the incidence of anthrax in some countries may be unrealistic.

7 Significant outbreaks of human infection have, however, been recorded in many countries where contact has been with the animals directly, or indirectly from

Factories Act (1895)

Anthrax notifications

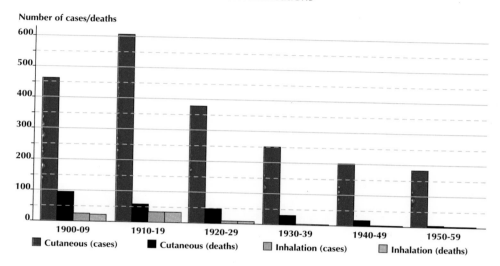

OPCS Public Health Act 1960

Anthrax notifications

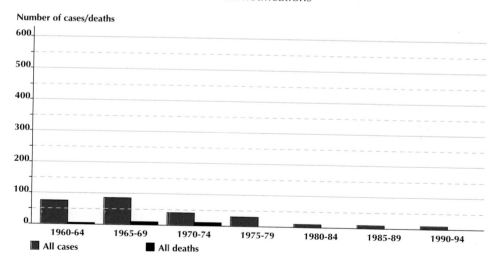

Figure 1: Human anthrax - England and Wales 1900-94

industrial processing of infected animal products, or working in environments contaminated by infected animals. Figure 2 shows a diagrammatic representation of worldwide incidence of the disease.

8   Overall, although disease reports give a broad indication of the incidence of anthrax globally, the system of notification may be subject to significant under-reporting and may not present an accurate picture. A low incidence of the disease exists in many developed countries and it is approaching eradication point or optimal control in others.

Table 1: Reported cases of human and animal anthrax in Britain 1989-96

Year	Human notifications*	Incidents	Animal Deaths Animals	Number†
1989	1	3	Cattle	3
	-	1	Pigs	19
1990	3	5	Cattle	6
1991	1	2	Cattle	2
1992	1	2	Cattle	2
1993	0	2	Cattle	5
1994	0	3	Cattle	5
1995	1	1	Cattle	1
		1	Ferrets	2
1996	0	2	Cattle	3

*No deaths reported

†Confirmed cases and not including animals which were treated and lived

Sources: **Human:** notifications and reports to OPCS, SCIEH and HSE

Animal: CVO reports (MAFF)

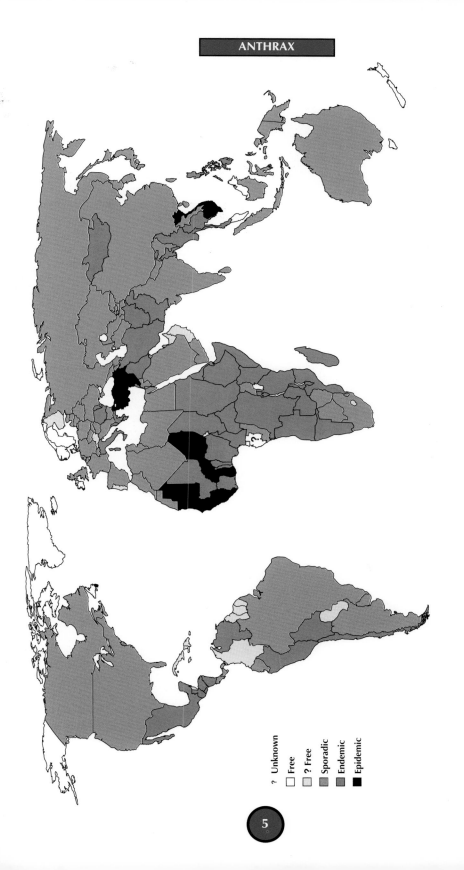

ANTHRAX

? Unknown

☐ Free

☐ ? Free

Sporadic

Endemic

■ Epidemic

Figure 2: Global livestock anthrax in 1994

OCCUPATIONS AND PROCESSES WHERE ANTHRAX PRESENTS A RISK

When can anthrax exposure occur?

9   Occupational exposure to anthrax may occur in those who:

▼ are in *contact with infected animals;*

▼ work with *materials or products from infected animals;*

▼ work on *land contaminated by infected animals or industrial processes involving infected animals.*

10 Table 2 shows the occupational association of human anthrax cases in England and Wales between 1975 and 1996.

Table 2: Human anthrax: occupational details of cases in Britain 1975-1996

Year	Sex/age	Occupation/epidemiology
1975	M 20	Leather worker
	M 53	Purchaser/machine tool company: gardening*
	M 60	Leather worker/animal hides*
	M 39	Slaughterman/animal carcasses*
1976	M 31	Farmer*
	M 36	Machinist, carpet factory*
	M 40	Unemployed/handled dead cow*
	M 40	Tannery worker
1977	M 59	Cleaner at a hostel
	F 19	Wool twister*
	M 27	Abattoir worker
	M 17	Butcher

Year	Sex/age	Occupation/epidemiology
1978	-	nil
1979	M 49	Chargehand in leather workshop/animal hides
	M 35	Textile mechanic in leather workshop/animal hides
	M 30	Abattoir and farm worker/animal carcasses
1980	M 38	Farm worker - handled offal/animal by-products
1981	-	nil
1982	M 50	Slaughterman/animal carcasses
1983	-	nil
1984	M 46	Consultant engineer/animal skin from Zambia
	M NK	Engineer in carpet factory/wool from Pakistan
1985	M 48	Butcher/animal carcasses
	M NK	Fellmonger (sheep skins and guts)
1986	-	nil
1987	-	nil
1988	M 23	Slaughterman/cattle carcasses
	M 52	Vicar's wife/blackberry picking or clothing from developing countries
1989	M 41	Factory worker/fertiliser made from animal bone
1990	M 32	Textile machinist/imported cotton/wool/leather
	M NK	Administrator/no information
	NK	No information
1991	NK	No information
1992	M NK	Slaughterman/no information
1993	-	nil
1994	-	nil
1995	M 63	Casual labourer/handled leather
1996	-	nil

*Clinically proven case

Source: Notifications to OPCS/anthrax register/SCIEH

11 It should be emphasised, however, that in all the occupations listed the risk of occupationally-acquired anthrax is low. Introducing the preventive or control measures described later in the guidance has reduced what was in previous years a significant risk to minimum levels. Making an appropriate assessment of a particular process will determine the risk of acquiring anthrax at work.

Occupations dealing with infected animals

12 Workers dealing with infected animals where there may be a risk of occupationally acquired anthrax include:

▼ farm workers, eg livestock breeders/keepers, shepherds, dairy workers - from skin contact with, or inhalation of, spores from diseased animals, or during disposal of infected carcasses and slurry;

▼ veterinary surgeons - from treatment of infected animals;

▼ local authority workers - from disposal of infected carcasses;

▼ zoo keepers - as above;

▼ abattoir workers/butchers - from exposure to anthrax spores during preparation of animals for food and food products. Table 3 shows that there have been more cases of occupationally acquired anthrax in abattoir workers than any other group over the past 20 years.

Occupations involving processing of infected animal material

13 A variety of industrial processes present situations where workers may be at risk of acquiring anthrax. These include those who work with/in:

▼ textiles, eg goat hair, wool;

▼ leather, eg importers, tanners;

▼ rendering, eg glue, gelatine, tallow, bone processing;

▼ storage and distribution, eg docks, warehousing or transport of any of the above.

Table 3: Anthrax: reported occupations 1975-1996

Occupations	Number
Slaughterhouse/abattoir worker	7
Tannery/leather worker	5
Farmer/farm worker	2
Butcher	2
Engineer	1
Textile worker	1
Bone meal worker	1

14 It was in the **textile** industry that the first case of occupationally acquired anthrax was recorded in the UK in 1847 and the subsequent increase in incidence of the disease was attributed to the importation of alpaca and mohair (goat hair). Most cases from dealing with these finer wools were seen in the mills in Bradford and hence the disease became known as 'Bradford disease', or 'woolsorters' disease' as it was called by the workers.

15 Historically, woolsorters' disease was most frequently encountered in workers whose job was to open fleece bales and to feed the animal hair into process machinery, or separate the bales according to quality. However, the disease has also been reported in the later stages of processing. So, while the risk of contracting anthrax may be greatest in the early stages of animal hair treatment, cases have been encountered in carding, combing, drawing and spinning the hair. Table 2 shows that when looking at the incidence of anthrax in the textile industry, cases have been recorded in wool twisters and machinists in carpet manufacture.

16 The importing of horse hair for the stuffing of mattresses and upholstery, and brush manufacture is now thought to be minimal. However, any contaminated imports not adequately treated by, eg, disinfection may present a risk of anthrax infection.

17 In the **leather** industry material is usually tanned before importation and the risk of occupationally acquiring anthrax is most significant in the handling of raw hides and skins in tanneries. Where treatment of dry and dry salted hides and skins is carried out, the early stages of processing are where the most significant risks of exposure may exist.

18 Anthrax contamination of **bones** imported for bone powder and bone charcoal production and the manufacture of animal feed, glue and gelatine may provide a risk to workers. Reports have described outbreaks in livestock after using contaminated cattle feed and fertiliser imports from countries where anthrax is endemic.

19 The reduction of raw bone processing in the UK, including the prohibition of mammalian meat and bone meal use for fertilisers and feedstuffs (as a BSE control measure), and the disinfection of bone products prior to importation has significantly reduced the risk of handling any contaminated material. In gelatine manufacture, anthrax spores are unlikely to survive the hydrochloric acid treatment used for bone demineralisation and so the process itself will probably destroy any contamination. Similarly, the steam pressures and temperatures used in **rendering** processes are likely to destroy any anthrax organisms present.

20 Workers in **storage and distribution** industries at, eg, docks, warehouses and in transport may be exposed to anthrax spores from infected material in the packaging they handle or directly from any contaminated products. Unprocessed material, eg animal hair that has been removed, packed and exported without further treatment, may require a veterinary check by the Ministry of Agriculture, Fisheries and Food (MAFF) under the terms of the Animal Origin (Import and Export) Regulations 1996. These checks are not required for processed material.

Occupations dealing with the contaminated environment

21 Various occupational groups may be at risk of coming into contact with anthrax spores and so be prone to incidental exposure. **Construction workers** may be at risk in a number of situations including:

▼ development of buildings on, eg, an old burial site of anthrax-infected carcasses or at an old tannery where there may be a risk of soil contamination;

▼ crypt clearances involving the opening of coffins containing people who have died of anthrax;

▼ demolition of old buildings. There may be a risk of anthrax spore contamination where infected animal hair was used to bind the plaster of walls.

22 Table 3 shows, however, that **no** cases of anthrax in construction workers have been reported in the last 20 years and so the risk of acquiring the disease is therefore very low.

ASSESSING THE RISK

Aims of assessment

23 Assessing risk for the purpose of complying with the Control of Substances Hazardous to Health Regulations 1994 (COSHH) means more than merely determining the likelihood of anthrax infection occurring at work. The final purpose of the assessment is to enable decisions to be made about the actions needed to prevent or control the risk. This includes the setting up of practical control measures, providing information and training, monitoring exposure and carrying out health surveillance where the assessment shows that these are required. Detailed advice on the assessment of risks for each occupational group is given later in the guidance.

Definition of terms

24 In making the assessment, it is helpful to appreciate the difference between **hazard** and **risk:**

▼ **hazard** may be defined as the intrinsic danger associated with the nature of an object, a substance, an activity, or in the context of this guidance, the *B.anthracis* micro-organism;

▼ **risk** means the probability that under certain circumstances, the hazard will be realised. In this context, this means the likelihood of exposure and subsequent occurrence of anthrax infection.

Conducting the assessment

25 Various factors need to be considered in assessing risk as required by COSHH. The key points are:

▼ **where** the anthrax organism may be present, eg in an intact animal or raw/processed products;

▼ **how** employees may be exposed, eg direct skin contact and/or inhalation;

▼ **what effects** it may have, eg development of cutaneous or inhalation anthrax;

▼ **estimate of exposure,** ie number and range of sources and frequency of contact, taking into account the systems of work and protective measures in use.

Analysis of each of the separate tasks that make up the work allows a systematic approach to assessment of where risks lie and what control measures are appropriate for each situation. All parts of the work process and the roles of the individuals in it should be examined closely.

Who is at risk?

26 Wherever there is the possibility of contact with anthrax-contaminated material or diseased animals, there is some risk of infection. The extent of the risk will depend on the:

▼ **frequency** and **duration** of contact;

▼ **extent** of contamination of the material or disease status of the animal;

▼ **effectiveness** of the control measures used.

27 It is important to recognise that not all exposures will result in infection. With proper regard to the risk assessment and the use of adequate controls, the likelihood of contracting anthrax will be minimised.

CONTROL MEASURES AGAINST ANTHRAX INFECTION

General measures applicable to all exposed populations

28 A number of protective measures are listed below which apply to occupations where there may be a risk of anthrax infection. Some of these precautions may not be relevant to all work situations and you should adapt and apply them to local circumstances. Take account too of any potential exposure to people other than those directly engaged in the work activity, eg members of the public, and other workers not directly involved:

▼ use good basic hygiene practices including regular hand-washing and avoid hand to mouth/eye etc contact;

▼ take rest breaks, including meals and drinks, in separate accommodation away from the workplace;

▼ cover all cuts, abrasions and other breaks in the skin with waterproof dressings and/or gloves;

▼ ensure first-aid equipment is available and regularly maintained;

▼ avoid personal contamination by the use of suitable protective clothing and ensure its safe decontamination /disposal;

▼ use separate storage for keeping protective clothing apart from personal clothing which is not worn during working hours;

▼ enclose processes as much as possible by use of engineering controls;

▼ exhaust airflows away from workers' breathing zone;

▼ use mechanical lifting aids where practicable to reduce direct handling;

▼ ensure high standards of cleanliness where appropriate with regular decontamination of work surfaces;

▼ dispose of contaminated waste safely;

▼ ensure adequate information, instruction and training on likelihood of infection and the control measures to be used;

▼ carry an anthrax medical card (for example MSB3 - contact HSE Books for details; see back cover) as a reminder of protective measures and an indicator of disease symptoms;

▼ provide suitable, regular, health surveillance arrangements where applicable;

▼ provide immunisation where appropriate.

Immunisation as a protection measure

29 The need for immunisation will be determined as part of the risk assessment. But it should only be used as a supplement to reinforce the procedural controls and use of protective equipment. Health and safety law requires that employees are not charged for vaccines offered as a means of protecting them at work. In providing vaccines, employers should ensure that employees are aware of the advantages and disadvantages of immunisation and its limitations. Adequate records should be kept of any immunisation provided.

30 The effectiveness of anthrax immunisation is difficult to quantify because of the decline in disease incidence due to both improved general hygiene measures and engineering controls. Limited studies have suggested the vaccine is effective although immunity is thought to require regular boosting.

31 The immunisation procedure involves four intra-muscular injections over an eight-month period. Annual boosters are recommended and the vaccine is available from the Public Health Laboratory Service (PHLS).

Control measures in the handling of infected animals

32 Occupational groups at risk may include farm workers, veterinary surgeons, zoo keepers, abattoir workers and butchers.

Farm workers, veterinary surgeons, zoo keepers

33 Much of the decline in the incidence of anthrax in humans is due to the corresponding decline in numbers of infected animals. This is because of the implementation of a successful livestock immunisation programme. However, when anthrax disease outbreaks do occur in animals it is necessary to carry out a number of preventive measures alongside the general controls listed in paragraph 28. This will ensure that infection is not spread to humans.

34 If a veterinary surgeon confirms an animal has died from anthrax, it is probable that it will have contaminated its immediate environment with its secretions and any slurry will need to be decontaminated. The State Veterinary Service of MAFF, in consultation with the local authority, will specify the action to take in decontaminating and disposing of the carcass.This is usually by incineration. The following points will assist in controlling the risk of spread of infection:

▼ segregate all other livestock from the affected areas and arrange for veterinary treatment as appropriate;

▼ implement general control measures; in particular use suitable protective clothing, ie waterproof coveralls and gloves, rubber boots, respiratory protection (eg fine dust filter mask or power-assisted visor);

▼ decontaminate affected land with either a suitable disinfectant - ensuring proper concentration for use and adequate contact time, or any other appropriate method, eg flaming;

▼ disinfect infected slurry by addition of suitable disinfectant; if, for example, formalin is used, then the concentrated (40%) solution should be pumped into the tank to make a final concentration of 4% in the mixture - adequate contact time (up to four days) should be allowed for the anthrax spores to be killed;

▼ dispose of disinfected slurry in consultation with MAFF by, eg, spreading onto arable land, or incineration after freezing;

▼ as part of the COSHH assessment the potential for human exposure to formaldehyde vapour should be considered. Formaldehyde is subject to a Maximum Exposure Limit (MEL) of 2 ppm over any 15 minute working period and also over an 8 hour working day. In addition to waterproof clothing, face and respiratory protection with an appropriate organic vapour filter or power-assisted equipment may be required. One conclusion from the COSHH assessment may be that it would be appropriate to enlist the services of a competent professional contractor to carry out the disinfection procedure.

Abattoir workers and butchers

35 To ensure no anthrax-infected material enters the food chain, slaughtering of infected livestock for human or animal consumption should not be carried out. The State Veterinary Service or Divisional Veterinary Manager of MAFF must be informed if there is any indication that an anthrax-infected animal has been received in the abattoir. The essential principles of good hygiene practice and the safe use of sharp instruments and tools apply throughout the slaughterhouse and butchery business. If an anthrax-infected carcass is ever encountered, then appropriate decontamination procedures will need to be implemented.

Control measures in rendering processes

36 The rendering industry receives animal waste from the abattoir, butcher and knackery and therefore would not expect to receive any infected material. Much of the rendering process is enclosed and the cooking stages use temperatures in excess of 130°C for approximately 30 minutes so any spores that might be present should be destroyed.

If contaminated animal waste was ever received then the general principles of good hygiene control apply during the initial transfer of waste to process filling points.

37 Bones or bonemeal imported from anthrax endemic areas for, eg, gelatine, glue and bone charcoal manufacture may present a risk of occupationally-acquired anthrax. However, only one case (in 1989) has been reported in the last 20 years. Importers of potentially contaminated material should assure themselves that consignments arrive with a 'sterilisation certificate' to attest that the products have been suitably heat-treated to kill any anthrax spores that may be present. Heat treatment by steam disinfection or autoclaving at 121°C for 15 minutes will be sufficient to sterilise or satisfactorily destroy the numbers of any anthrax spores in the material. Allowance should be made for the steam to penetrate all the material being autoclaved. Monitoring of this may be carried out by placing test probes or thermocouples at various parts of a load to check actual temperatures achieved.

38 The general control measures described in paragraph 28 will also be applicable in considering the risk assessment of any anthrax contamination in a bone/bonemeal consignment.

Control measures in the textile industry

39 The risk of textile workers acquiring anthrax, although low, is most significant during the initial handling of contaminated material, eg transportation for storage, opening bales and sorting. Good practice to control any exposure to anthrax usually involves washing (scouring) and disinfection of the raw material before any processing for consumer products manufacture. Consider the appropriate use of engineering controls at the initial stages described in paragraphs 41-42 alongside the general measures quoted in paragraph 28.

Assessment of raw material contamination

40 It may be difficult to assess what level of contamination, if any, is present in a consignment of raw material. Because of this it may be helpful to find out the prevalence of anthrax in the country of the material's origin. Further information on the assessment process and the methods available to sample and test for the presence of anthrax spores can be found in Appendix 3.

Engineering controls

41 Untreated textile materials should be segregated from 'clean' or disinfected goods to avoid cross-contamination with anthrax spores.

42 General ventilation requirements of segregated areas should be assessed to control the level of airborne contamination (ie anthrax spores in dust). Similarly local exhaust ventilation (LEV) should be employed at points of worker contact with potential sources of anthrax contamination. With any LEV system the aim is to control the release of the dust by capturing it as close as possible to the place where it is generated.

Decontamination/disinfection

43 Where textile materials are suspected of containing anthrax spores a system of effective decontamination or disinfection will need to be in place. A number of chemical disinfectants are known to kill anthrax spores, for example, formalin, chlorine, hydrogen peroxide, peracetic acid, methyl bromide, and ethylene oxide. Physical decontamination using radiation or autoclaving and a combination of both chemical and physical methods, for example formalin and steam, have been used to treat raw material.

44 The use of a formalin solution has invariably been the method of choice for disinfecting animal hair suspected of being contaminated with anthrax spores. Material is first scoured with detergent to free infected material from matted hair and any bound animal excreta or blood. It is then immersed in a formalin bath and finally passed through a heat drying process where residual formaldehyde vapour continues its disinfecting action. Extensive research has been carried out by HSE on this method and Appendix 3 gives more information on the efficacy of using formalin as a disinfectant and the importance of monitoring the treatment process.

Control measures in the leather industry

45 The risk of leather industry workers acquiring anthrax is, as in the textile industry, most significant during the initial stages of handling potentially contaminated material. If raw hides/skins are contaminated with anthrax spores, the most significant risk will be handling them before tanning. The general control principles listed in paragraph 28 therefore apply, together with appropriate segregation of untreated hides and skins, and use of, where appropriate, ventilation control, as described in paragraphs 41-42.

46 As part of the tanning process itself, strong alkali liming of raw skins followed by neutralisation in an acid bath will kill or significantly reduce the numbers of any anthrax spores present. Table 3 does show, however, that instances of anthrax have resulted from working with tanned leather. This underlines the need to prevent cross-contamination in storage between untreated and treated materials. However, appropriate methods of sampling and testing may also be relevant to establish how successful any disinfection regime is. Some of the chemical disinfectants referred to in paragraph 43 may be of further use when decontaminating the tannery storage areas.

Control measures in the development of contaminated land

47 Redevelopment of sites previously occupied by industrial premises where there might have been a risk of anthrax contamination in, eg, old farms, anthrax burial sites, tanneries and woollen mills, or where old buildings due for demolition have hair plaster walls, or crypt clearance work, may present an incidental risk to construction workers.

48 Appropriate soil sampling/building material sampling, and laboratory testing for anthrax **may** give an indication of spore population and their distribution at a site. It is, however, better to adopt a precautionary approach if redeveloping industrial sites, and assume that anthrax spores **are** likely to be present **although probably at low numbers which would not put the worker at significant risk.** Appropriate assessment needs to be taken of the intended use of any site being redeveloped and any remedial action thought necessary. If decontamination is required the best practical option may be heat treatment, which normally means incineration. If the area is too large, chemical disinfection may be more appropriate.

49 The general control measures described in paragraph 28 will need to be applied, paying particular attention to:

▼ good hygiene practice;
▼ proper welfare facilities;
▼ use of suitable personal protective equipment;
▼ information, instruction and training on anthrax, the relevance of immunisation and first-aid requirements.

APPENDIX 1: HEALTH AND SAFETY LAW AND OTHER RELEVANT LEGISLATION

The Health and Safety at Work etc Act 1974 (HSWA)

1   All work except domestic service is subject to regulation under the Health and Safety at Work etc Act 1974. Employers, employees and the self-employed have specific duties to protect, so far as is reasonably practicable, those at work and those who may be affected by their work activity.

The Control of Substances Hazardous to Health Regulations 1994 (COSHH)

2   COSHH provides a comprehensive framework for controlling risk from most hazardous substances, including biological agents. The anthrax micro-organism, *Bacillus anthracis,* is a biological agent as defined in COSHH.

3   COSHH requires employers to assess the risk of all infectious agents, including anthrax, for both their employees and others who may be affected by their work, for example, members of the public. When a risk has been established, employers then need to select appropriate control measures, to ensure that they are properly used. Any protective equipment used must be regularly examined for defects, thoroughly maintained and kept in safe storage when not in use. In addition, employees must receive suitable information, instruction and training on the risks they may encounter at work. Subject to assessment, there may also be a need to provide vaccination for employees and make arrangements for suitable health surveillance.

The Management of Health and Safety at Work Regulations 1992 (MHSW)

4   The duties of MHSW, because of their more wide-ranging nature, overlap with other health and safety legislation. Like COSHH, MHSW requires, for example, an assessment of risks to health, provision of health surveillance (where appropriate) and

information for employees. However, there are some other equally important requirements in MHSW not appearing in COSHH and these need to be addressed in protecting workers. Therefore, the two sets of Regulations must be observed. However, where there is a clear overlap, compliance with the duty in the more specific regulation will normally be sufficient to meet the corresponding requirement of the other set of Regulations. For example, COSHH requires employers and the self-employed to assess the risk arising from substances hazardous to health and so includes those risks of acquiring anthrax infection. Therefore, the COSHH assessment will not need to be repeated for the purpose of the MHSW risk assessment, although other issues may have to be considered.

Local safety policies and codes of practice

5   Where any risks to health and safety are known to exist, it is essential that most employers have a safety policy (see S.2(3) HSWA). While the policy statement may deal in general terms with an employer's intent to develop and maintain a safe working environment, more specific information on the arrangements for working safely day-to-day is best provided in local codes of practice. All staff, including all newcomers, must be made aware of them. Managers have a responsibility to make the policy and codes freely accessible, either by putting them on display or by giving them to all staff. Instruction on the day-to-day application of the code of practice is needed to make it work effectively.

6   A local code of practice should reflect the principles expressed in law, in this or other official guidance, and should also be tailored specifically to local circumstances. Accident reporting procedures, for example, should show clearly who in the establishment to contact.

7   Periodic review of local codes should be undertaken and it is appropriate to monitor performance in their application. By identifying unsafe practices highlighted, for example, by accident reports and safety audits, further incidents may be avoided. The assessment of risk required by COSHH will need to be reviewed regularly and revised when conditions change, or an incident occurs, or any deficiency is noted.

Information, instruction and training of employees

8 Both COSHH and MHSW require that employees receive appropriate information, instruction and training on any identifiable risks to their health arising from work. There is a need to ensure a clear understanding by all concerned of the actions to take when dealing with situations in which exposure may occur. They must be informed of the precautions to take to avoid or minimise those risks. The local codes of practice form part of this process of information.

9 Occupational health staff or advisers, where available, have a key role in providing information on risks to health from work and in developing suitable training material. For example, the HSE anthrax carry card, MSB3 (contact HSE Books for details - see back cover), should be distributed to employees who may be exposed to anthrax at work.

10 COSHH also requires that employers provide information on the results of any monitoring of exposure and on the collective results of any health surveillance undertaken in accordance with regulation 11.

Health surveillance

11 Where it is appropriate for the protection of the health of employees, both COSHH and MHSW require that employees are under suitable health surveillance when '...*there is a reasonable likelihood that the disease or effect may occur under the particular conditions of this work and there are valid techniques for detecting indications of the disease or the effect*'. This may be by, for example, regular checking of the skin for the first signs of anthrax infection. If unexplained swellings are visible then a doctor or occupational health adviser should be consulted immediately. It will also be appropriate to set up and maintain a health record.

The Reporting of Incidents, Diseases and Dangerous Occurrences Regulations 1995 (RIDDOR)

12 These recently revised Regulations are designed to provide a national record of certain types of injury, diseases and dangerous occurrences that might jeopardise the health and safety of workers. There is a requirement in RIDDOR for employers to report acute illness requiring medical treatment, where there is reason to believe that this resulted from an exposure to a pathogen or infected material. This will include any case of anthrax contracted at work.

The Public Health (Infectious Diseases) Regulations 1988

13 Anthrax was made a notifiable disease under an earlier version of these Regulations in 1960. Further information may be obtained from a local authority.

Industrial injury benefit

14 Under the Social Security Act 1975 anthrax is a prescribed industrial disease. Further information may be obtained from a Social Security office.

Animal Origin (Import and Export) Regulations 1996

15 The Animal Origin (Import and Export) Regulations 1996 implement the Balai Products Directive (92/118) and lay down animal health and public health requirements governing trade in and imports into the European Community of products of animal origin not subjected to the requirements of other veterinary check directives.

Anthrax Prevention Order (APO) 1971 and APO 1971 (Exemptions) Regulations 1982

16 The Anthrax Prevention Order (APO) 1971 prohibits or places conditions on the importation of animal hair products declared *'likely to be infected with anthrax'*. The associated Anthrax Prevention Order (Exemptions) Regulations 1982 (APO(E) Regulations) enable HSE to exempt any person(s) or any goods of any description from any requirement or prohibition imposed by the APO, provided that the health and safety of those likely to be affected would not be prejudiced. Under the APO and APO(E) Regulations, consignments of otherwise prohibited goods undergo disinfection by an approved process (see Appendix 3 and paragraph 44 in the main text for more details).

Ministry of Agriculture, Fisheries and Food (MAFF) legislation

17 Relevant legislative requirements for notification of diseased animals, remedial precautionary actions to be followed and the role of the MAFF veterinary inspector include:

▼ the Anthrax Order 1991;
▼ the Anthrax (Amendment) Order 1996;
▼ the Diseases of Animals (Approved Disinfectants) Order 1978;
▼ the Diseases of Animals (Approved Disinfectants) (Amendment) Order 1978;
▼ the Diseases of Animals (Approved Disinfectants) (Amendment) Order 1994.

Carriage of Dangerous Goods by Road and Rail (Classification, Packaging and Labelling) Regulations (CDGCPL) 1994

18 Arrangements for the domestic carriage of goods contaminated with anthrax material may place duties on employers for the classification, packaging and labelling of those goods.

APPENDIX 2: CLINICAL FEATURES OF ANTHRAX

Cutaneous anthrax

1   At the point of infection a lesion appears on the skin as a small pimple or painless swelling which, within three to four days, produces a ring of blisters with increased swelling. After five to seven days this ulcerates to form a necrotic black centre or 'eschar'. This swells further, extending some distance from the original lesion. The mature lesion is described as a 'malignant pustule' because of its characteristic appearance. After ten days the eschar begins to heal, although it takes up to six weeks to completely clear up. Without treatment, in a small proportion of cases, infection may spread to the bloodstream and produce disease effects similar to other types of anthrax.

Inhalation anthrax

2   Airborne particles containing *B.anthracis* spores pass through the respiratory tract and are deposited in the base of the lungs where they are taken up by the immune system. Initial symptoms are similar to those of influenza. When passed to the lymphoid tissue, the spores germinate, multiply, and produce a powerful toxin. The original mild symptoms may then develop rapidly into difficulty in breathing, skin discolouration and disorientation, leading to coma and death within 24 hours.

3   Inhalation anthrax has been reported in the past in the woollen industry and was known as 'woolsorters' disease'.

Ingestion anthrax

4   While commonly a route of infection in animals, ingestion anthrax is rare in humans and there is no record of its occurrence in the UK. It is most often seen in parts of Africa and is caused by eating undercooked meat from infected animals. When the meat is consumed, the individual may suffer initially with stomach pain and diarrhoea. Fever, coma and eventually death may develop within a few hours of the onset of these symptoms.

Treatment

5   Early diagnosis of individuals infected with anthrax, and prompt therapy, can result in a quick recovery. Almost all strains of *B.anthracis* are highly sensitive to penicillin and this provides the basis for treatment in most parts of the world. In severely affected individuals, and in cases where inhalation or ingestion anthrax is suspected, symptomatic treatment in addition to antibiotic therapy can prevent the development of a fatal infection.

Infectivity in humans

6   The infectivity of *B.anthracis* for humans is generally regarded as low. This is based on the very large volume of potentially infected raw materials that have been imported in the past and the relative rarity of infection. Studies have described workers inhaling more than 1000 anthrax spores during a working day with a low incidence of the disease. Other reports have shown the isolation of *B.anthracis* in the nose and throat of healthy, unvaccinated workers. Infectivity may also depend on the virulence of the infecting anthrax strain and the individual's state of health. Conversely, cases have been reported where workers **have** had minimal exposure.

APPENDIX 3: ASSESSING AND CONTROLLING ANTHRAX RISKS IN THE IMPORTATION, TRANSPORT AND STORAGE OF TEXTILE FIBRES

Introduction

1   This information here is intended to assist companies and individuals who import, transport, store and process anthrax risk textile materials such as goat hair originating from countries where an anthrax infection exists.

Scope

2   The information here is based on the principles of the Anthrax Prevention Order (APO) which currently regulates the importation of a proportion of these materials. Control of anthrax in the workplace is now exercised under COSHH which applies to employers and self-employed people, who have duties towards employees and other people who may be affected by their acitivities. The information in this Appendix should assist those who have to assess and control risks under regulations 6-12 of COSHH and should be read in conjunction with paragraphs 39-44 of the main text.

Risk assessment

3   Unless each consignment is tested for anthrax (see below) the hazard may be estimated on the basis of the type and source of the material. Hazard categories are defined as follows.

▼ **A** Goat hair, including cashmere and mohair from Iran, Iraq, Afghanistan (and other Central Asian republics), India, Pakistan, Bangladesh, and Africa (except South Africa). Goat hair excluding cashmere (except South Africa) and common goat hair from China and Mongolia.

▼ **B** Goat hair, including cashmere and mohair from Russia, Central and South America, South Africa, Spain, Italy, Greece, and Turkey; cashmere and mohair from China and Mongolia; sheep's wool from Hazard A countries (not China or Mongolia).

▼ **C** Animal hair from Australia, New Zealand, USA and Europe (except countries mentioned above). Hair includes alpaca, camel, goat (mohair and cashmere and common goat hair), angora and vicuna.

These hazard categories relate to recent (1995) knowledge and are **not** inclusive. World occurrence of anthrax is likely to change with time, and risk assessments should reflect these changes. Information on the current picture may be available through HSE's InfoLine (see back cover for details).

4 Assessment of risks under regulation 6 of COSHH needs to take into account the infection status, if known, or the hazard category of the material, and where and how the material is handled. Table 4 will assist importers, transport and warehousing companies and processors in assessing risks to their own staff, the public and their customers.

Table 4

Hazard category (undisinfected material)	Purchasing in country of origin	Transport of bales - by road/air/sea	Warehousing and storage	Opening and manual sorting	Scouring	Processing - carding, spinning, after scouring without disinfection
A	High	Low	Medium	High	Medium	Medium
B	Low	Low	Low	Medium	Low	Low
C	Negligible	Negligible	Negligible	Negligible or low	Negligible	Negligible

It is assumed that processing (eg carding, spinning etc) is carried out on scoured material. Detergent scouring (even without disinfection) reduces the risk in later processing. Therefore those importing material in top, noils or yarn form will need to know if the raw material was scoured before they can assess the risk.

Assessing the overall risk

5   The risk to people may be regarded as the product of three factors:

$$\begin{array}{ccccccc} \textit{Probability or degree of} & & \textit{Process factors} & & \textit{Precautions} & & \\ & \mathbf{X} & & \mathbf{X} & & = & \textit{Overall risk} \\ \textit{infection in raw material} & & \textit{(see Table 4)} & & \textit{against anthrax} & & \end{array}$$

It is expected that most importers and purchasers will seek assurance that the probability of infection is zero, or as low as possible, as process factors are largely fixed (ie they are determined by end use). So the need for precautions can be thereby reduced or eliminated, allowing the material to be handled like any other textile fibre. If processors wish to use material with a finite infection hazard their assessments and precautions will need to take account of this - see paragraphs 23-49 of the main text.

Reducing the infection hazard

Hazard A materials

6   It is recommended that Hazard A materials in the raw state (ie unscoured) should always be disinfected. It should be noted that undisinfected hair is subject to the requirements of the Animal Origin (Import and Export) Regulations 1996* and the Anthrax Prevention Order (APO).

7   If disinfected according to a previously validated method (see paragraphs 18-27) these materials may be brought into the UK in the ordinary way, ie in compliance with normal import restrictions.

---

*   The Animal Origin (Import and Export) Regulations implemented the Balai Products Directive and came into force on 1 January 1997 and require veterinary checks/documentation for unprocessed animal products entering the European Community from third countries. Further advice on the Regulations should be obtained from MAFF.

8 If disinfected outside the European Union these materials may be imported into the UK but should be segregated from other commodities, or sealed in plastic film. While still wrapped or segregated, samples should be taken and tested for anthrax. On receipt of a clear result the goods may be released for processing.

Hazard B materials

9 Hazard B materials may be imported in the raw state if accompanied by a certificate of origin in the case of Chinese cashmere/mohair or in the case of other Hazard B materials by a foreign test certificate.* Where material is imported from a known dependable source a valid veterinary certificate and certificate of origin may be acceptable. If reliable documentation is not available these materials should be tested in the UK.

Hazard C materials

10 Hazard C materials may be imported unrestricted, providing that there is documentary proof of the country of origin.

Segregation

Transport

11 It is recommended that undisinfected Hazard A material, and material whose documentation has not been validated, should be transported in a dedicated freight container, or other segregated containment, ie it should not share a load-carrying space with other commodities. An exception to this can be made if bales are sealed in plastic wrapping, but this may be suitable only for journeys of short duration due to problems with condensation inside wrappings (sweating). Segregation of air freighted material is difficult to achieve and it is recommended that this is always individually wrapped and sealed.

---

*   *While the APO remains in force, application must be made to the HSE Office in Leeds for import certification on certain goods, eg goat hair.*

Storage and handling

12 Undisinfected Hazard A material, and material whose documentation has not been validated, should be stored separately in a designated area. There should be no physical contact with other commodities and storage should be in a marked area at least two metres from other stacks. It is advised that this material should not be manually handled, but that lift trucks with clamps, or similar, should be used. The area should be marked to indicate that there may be an infection risk.

Sampling and testing

13 Where sampling and testing is indicated in paragraphs 8-9 (for certain Hazard A and B materials) a sample should be taken from 10% of bales, with a minimum of two being sampled. If a consignment consists of a single bale then one sample is sufficient.

14 The person taking samples should wear protective gloves, a disposable respirator (type P2 or P3) and, if contamination of clothing is foreseeable, disposable coveralls (eg if entering a freight container). Immunisation is strongly recommended. The samples should be placed in a sealed bag and labelled with the bale number, date and shipment details. Where two or more consignments are shipped together, samples should be taken from each.

15 Samples bags should be double bagged and placed in a strong package and taken, or posted (in containers complying with Post Office guidance) to a competent laboratory where bacteriological tests specific to *B.anthracis* should be performed.

16 If a positive result is found the whole batch or consignment should be disinfected or returned to the consignor.

Documentation

17 It is often difficult to assess the reliability of documentation from abroad, when little information is available on test methods, criteria or quality control. Four types of certificate are generally available.

▼ **Certificate of Origin.** This is self-explanatory but is sometimes issued in the country where the material is scoured (eg China, Egypt).

▼ **Veterinary Certificate.** This may certify that the animals or area from which the material has come is free of anthrax.

▼ **Disinfection Certificate.** This certifies that the material has undergone a disinfection process, which is usually specified, eg formalin treatment or fumigation.

▼ **Test Certificate.** This may certify that samples have been taken and tested by bacteriological culture, and have been found free of anthrax.

If documents have not come from a known reliable source or there are other reasons not to trust them, testing should be carried out in the UK by the Public Health Laboratory Service (PHLS) or other competent laboratory. Documents should be retained for two years after processing has been completed.

Disinfection

18 Different methods of disinfection are available. These will kill spores, but in commercial use cannot be guaranteed to be 100% effective. However, if operated correctly they will reduce the number of spores to a safe level. The following methods are available. The use of formalin, steam and irradiation have been previously validated.

Formalin

19 The material is passed through six bowls of a wool scouring set. The first five bowls provide normal scouring conditions, ie the first bowl contains a solution of sodium carbonate, the second and third contain nonylphenol decaethylene glycol (detergent) at 46°C, regulated automatically to 0.7-1% of the weight of the material. In the fourth and fifth bowls the material is rinsed with a continuous feed of fresh water. The sixth bowl provides disinfection and contains 0.9% formaldehyde solution at 43°C. The concentration of formaldehyde is maintained by an automatic dosing pump.

Residence time of the material in the formaldehyde bowl should be at least one minute, and no rinsing occurs before drying.

20 The material then passes through two conveyor driers. Temperature in the first is 70°C and in the second 90°C.

21 The hazardous properties of any chemical disinfectant will need to be assessed before its use. Formaldehyde is classified as toxic, a category 3 carcinogen, and is irritant to the eyes, upper respiratory passages and skin. It is subject to a Maximum Exposure Limit (MEL) of 2 ppm and so personal exposures must be reduced to as low a level as reasonably practicable. The exposure limit refers to both an 8 hour time weighted average (TWA) period and a 15 minute short term (STEL) period and is readily exceeded without good engineering control.

Steam method

22 Disinfection is carried out according to the fractional diffusion process (vacuum-steam-vacuum, VSV). The material need not be loosened but any impermeable wrappings should be removed and temperatures should be measured by positioning thermocouples in the centre of bales. Drying after disinfection takes place during the final vacuum phase.

23 The sequence of the phases is as follows.

▼ **First phase:** vacuum.

▼ **Second phase:** steam introduced until temperature reaches 102°C.

▼ **Third phase:** vacuum.

▼ **Fourth phase:** steam introduced until temperature reaches 104°C.

▼ **Fifth phase:** vacuum.

▼ **Sixth phase:** steam introduced until temperature reaches 105°C.

▼ **Seventh phase:** vacuum.

▼ **Eighth phase:** steam introduced until temperature reaches 112°C. Temperature held for 20 minutes.

▼ **Ninth phase:** drying.

Irradiation

24 Disinfection should be achieved by exposure to gamma radiation from a cobalt 60 source to a minimum total dose of 41.5 kGy and validated by quantitative radiation dosimetry.

Fumigation (not validated)

25 Fumigation is not recommended, due to the difficulty in ensuring that the fumigant can penetrate clumps of hair from the opened bale, spores trapped in raw greasy material, or dried clots of blood or faeces.

Quality control

26 Importers of animal hair will want to assure themselves that disinfection has been carried out satisfactorily and should ask for documentary evidence of this. The parameters of the process should be checked frequently (eg concentration, immersion time, temperature) and recorded.

27 Whatever method is used, it should be tested periodically by putting seeded samples through the process, eg, using *Bacillus subtilis var. globigii*, a harmless spore-forming organism similar to anthrax. Also, it is recommended that raw material taken before and after the process should be tested periodically for contamination.

Health surveillance and immunisation

28 Immunisation is strongly recommended for company representatives, such as buyers, who visit the countries of origin and handle hair which is potentially infected,

employees undertaking sampling and any other employees identified in the COSHH assessment as being at significant risk. Workers who may come into contact with potentially infected material such as fork truck drivers and hand sorters (plus buyers and samplers) should receive advice and instruction on the effects and signs of anthrax and be given an anthrax precautionary card. See paragraphs 28-49 of the main text for further information.

Printed and published by the Health and Safety Executive   C50   9/97